Wheels can be found in many sizes and forms

Wheels & Axles

John Hudson Tiner

A⁺

Smart Apple Media

COPYRIGHT

❏ Published by Smart Apple Media

1980 Lookout Drive, North Mankato, MN 56003

Designed by Rita Marshall

Printed in the United States of America

❏ Photographs by Richard Cummins, Galyn C. Hammond, The Image Finders (Jim Baron), Gunter Marx Photography, Paul T. McMahon, Tom Myers, John Perryman, D. Jeanene Tiner

❏ Library of Congress Cataloging-in-Publication Data

Tiner, John Hudson. Wheels and axles / by John Tiner. p. cm. — (Simple machines)

Includes bibliographical references.

Summary: Discusses wheels and axles and the ways in which they are used.

❏ ISBN 1-58340-137-7

1. Simple machines–Juvenile literature. 2. Wheels–Juvenile literature. 3. Axles–Juvenile literature. [1. Wheels. 2. Axles.] I. Title.

TJ147 .T498 2002   621.8'11–dc21   2001054164

❏ First Edition 9 8 7 6 5 4 3 2 1

Wheels & Axles

CONTENTS

The Wheel and Axle

In ancient times, people learned that rollers made it easier to move things. They put rollers under stone blocks to move them. Egyptians built the **pyramids** with the help of log rollers. ☐ A disk cut from a log makes a wheel. Ancient drawings show that the first use of a wheel was to make pottery. The wheel made a circular table. A potter turned it to spin clay to form pots. Later, wheels were put on wagons and chariots. ☐ A wheel is fastened to a central shaft called an axle. Each time the wheel turns, so does the axle. Usually the

axle is smaller than the wheel. One of the first uses of a **wheel**

and axle was to raise a bucket of water from a well. One end

of a rope was tied to the axle, and the other end was tied to

A potter's wheel is used to shape clay into pots

the bucket. Turning the wheel wound the rope around the

axle. The rope pulled up the bucket of water.

Wheels and Axles at Work

Sometimes a person is not strong enough to do a job

just by lifting or pulling. A wheel and axle can make the job

easier. Turning a screw into wood is made easier with a

screwdriver. A screwdriver is a wheel and axle. The handle is

the wheel, and the metal shaft is the axle. A twist of the handle

makes the shaft turn too, and the screw twists into the wood.

Machines exchange **effort** for distance. This means that a

job can be made easier (a smaller effort), but it usually takes

longer to do (a greater distance) as a result. For instance,

suppose a wheel is bigger than its axle. A person can turn the

A screwdriver is a basic kind of wheel and axle

A merry-go-round is a fun form of wheel

wheel fairly easily to wind a rope around the axle and lift a heavy load. But the wheel must be turned through a greater distance than that through which the load is lifted. ☐ A **windlass** is a type of wheel and axle used to lift a heavy load such as a large bucket of water from a well. Suppose the windlass makes the bucket seem 10 times lighter. A point on the wheel must go around 10 feet (3 m) for each foot (30.5 cm) that the bucket comes up.

Long ago, foods such as salted meat were shipped in barrels. It was easier to roll a barrel than carry a box.

Water wheels capture the energy of moving water

Gears

A gear is a wheel with teeth. The teeth of one gear fit in the gaps between the teeth on another gear. The gears do not have to be the same size. One gear may be large with many teeth. The other gear may be small with few teeth. The smaller one turns many times for each turn of the larger one. ☐ Some clocks have hour, minute, and second hands to show the time. Gears turn each hand of the clock at a different speed. The second hand has the smallest gear, so it turns the fastest. ☐ Some machines have gears that do not touch. Instead, a chain

connects one gear to another. For example, a bicycle has a

chain. It goes around the large gear at the pedal, then it runs

to the smaller gear at the back wheel.

Gears are wheels with teeth that fit together

The Bicycle

The wheel and axle is a **simple machine**. A bicycle is a muscle-powered machine. It is made of several simple machines, including the wheel and axle. The pedal wheel and the back wheel are gears. The pedal gear has twice as many teeth as the back gear. This means that a single turn of the pedal causes the back wheel to turn two times. ☐ A 10-speed bicycle has gears of different sizes to give

In some countries, bicycles are the main means of transportation. Bicycles use no fuel and do not pollute.

Gears can turn the wheels of a bicycle quickly or slowly

it more than one speed. On a level surface, a rider chooses a

higher (larger) gear. The rider pedals slowly, but the bicycle

moves at a fast pace. When the rider comes to a hill, a lower

(smaller) gear is better. In low gear, **A merry-go-round is a fun ride built on a huge wheel that spins. Children ride on seats that often are shaped like kinds of animals.**

the rider pedals more times for each

turn of the bicycle wheel. The rider

pedals faster and with less effort, but

the bicycle does not move as quickly. ☐ People have relied on

wheels and axles since ancient times. Bicycles, cars, clocks, and

Gears move the hands of a clock at different speeds

winches all use wheels and axles. Not all wheels and axles look the same, though. A key is also a kind of wheel and axle. The part a person holds is wide so the key is easier to turn. No matter where they are found, wheels and axles make our lives easier in many ways.

A key is a simple wheel and axle used to turn locks

A Gear Experiment

This experiment will show you how gears and a little effort make a bicycle travel far.

What You Need

A bicycle
Chalk

What You Do

1. Make a chalk mark that is easy to see on the side of the back wheel.
2. Ride the bike a short, set distance and count the number of times you turn the pedal. (One complete turn takes the same foot back to the same place.)
3. Have a friend watch the chalk mark on the back wheel and count the number of times the back wheel goes around as you ride.

What You See

How many times did the wheel go around for each turn of the pedal? Most bicycle wheels will go around about twice as many times as the pedal wheel. The bicycle gears multiply the distance you travel. A single turn of the pedal takes you farther than you could travel in a single step.

A bicycle uses several gears to make pedaling easier

INFORMATION

Index

Words to Know

effort (EH-fert)—the pushing or pulling force that moves a load

pyramids (PEER-uh-midz)—large stone monuments of ancient Egypt built over the tombs of kings

simple machine (SIM-pul mah-SHEEN)—a basic device that makes a job easier

wheel and axle (WEEL and AK-suhl)—a simple machine with a larger wheel connected to a smaller axle

windlass (WIND-less)—a machine for lifting; a rope winds around an axle when a wheel is turned

Read More

Dunn, Andrew. *Wheels at Work*. New York: Thomson Learning, 1993.

Seller, Mick. *Wheels, Pulleys and Levers*. New York: Shooting Star Press, 1995.

Whittle, Fran, and Sarah Lawrence. *Simple Machines*. Austin, Tex.: Raintree Steck-Vaughn, 1998.

Internet Sites

Learning Network Fact Monster:
Wheel and Axle
http://www.factmonster.com/ce6/
sci/A0852032.html

MIKIDS.COM: Wheels
http://www.mikids.com/SMachines
Wheels.htm

Simple Machine Page for Kids
http://www.san-marino.k12.ca.us/
~summer1/machines/
simplemachines.html